THE *floral* DECOUPAGE SOURCEBOOK

THE *floral* DECOUPAGE SOURCEBOOK

Jocasta Innes & Stewart Walton

Photography by Richard Foster

CONRAN OCTOPUS

To Roxy

First published in 1996 by
Conran Octopus Limited
37 Shelton Street
London WC2H 9HN

Text copyright © 1996 Paintability Ltd
Design copyright ©1996 Conran
Octopus Limited
Photography copyright © 1996
Richard Foster

Editorial Director *Suzannah Gough*
Senior Editor *Jenna Jarman*
Project Editor *Alison Bolus*
Designer *Alison Barclay*
Photographic Direction *Sue Storey*
Stylist *Tiffany Davies*
Picture Researcher *Rachel Davies*
Production Controller *Mano Mylvaganam*

A catalogue record for this book is available
from the British Library

ISBN 1 85029 840 8

Produced by Mandarin Offset Ltd.
Printed and bound in Hong Kong

PUBLISHER'S ACKNOWLEDGEMENTS
The publisher would like to thank the following for providing
props for photography:
Lunn Antiques, 86 New Kings Road, London, SW6
Paint Magic, 116 Sheen Road, Richmond, Surrey, TW9 1UR

PICTURE CREDITS
33 Earl of Derby Collection, Suffolk/Bridgeman Art Library;
35-47 Courtesy of the Board of Trustees of the Victoria & Albert
Museum/Angelo Hornak; **49** Christies, London/Bridgeman Art
Library; **51** Museum of Natural History, London/Bridgeman
Art Library; **53** Royal Botanical Gardens, Kew/Bridgeman Art Library;
55 Courtesy of the Board of Trustees of the Victoria & Albert
Museum/Bridgeman Art Library; **57** Mary Evans Picture Library;
59 Angelo Hornak; **61-69** Mary Evans Picture Library;
71-73 Angelo Hornak; **75-77** Mary Evans Picture Library;
79 Courtesy of the Board of Trustees of the Victoria & Albert
Museum/Bridgeman Art Library; **81** Courtesy of the Board of
Trustees of the Victoria & Albert Museum/Angelo Hornak;
83 Mary Evans Picture Library; **85** Bridgeman Art Library;
87 Mary Evans Picture Library; **89** above Courtesy of the Linnaean
Society Library/Angelo Hornak; **89** below Lindley Library, RHS,
London/Bridgeman Art Library; **91** above Chester Beatty Library and
Gallery of Oriental Art/Bridgeman Art Library; **91** below Bridgeman
Art Library; **93** Lindley Library, RHS, London/Bridgeman Art Library;
95 Mary Evans Picture Library.

Contents

INTRODUCTION

Take a printed image, cut out neatly, paste down on anything from trinket box to armoire, and you have worked a transformation. The beauty of decoupage (the word derives from the French word *decouper*: to cut out) is that it allows even the least artistically gifted to preen in borrowed plumage. Given deftness, patience and some eye-catching motifs, plus lots of varnish, anyone can make an ordinary object more interesting and attractive.

Decoupage first began to flourish in the late fifteenth century, when bold and elaborate printed decorative borders were produced in Germany for use on furniture, simulating the complex wood inlay, or 'tarsia' work, that was fashionable during the Renaissance. Glued down and heavily varnished, this printed short-cut was almost indistinguishable from the real thing, at least at a distance. Probably the subterfuge was reflected in the price. Certainly when the Venetians later began using tinted cut-outs of chinoiserie figures, swags and blossoms to enliven painted furniture in a lively approximation of much-prized Oriental lacquer wares, the process was explicitly seen as cut-price, and none the worse for that. Indeed, this light-hearted rip-off of the laborious effect of genuine Eastern lacquer was christened *arte povera* – the poor man's art. Ironically, surviving examples today change hands for astronomical prices! During the eighteenth century, decoupage joined such activities as bead work, straw work, watercolour painting and making music as suitable time-fillers and accomplishments for European gentlewomen. It is too easy to dismiss and patronize these 'ladies' amusements', as they came to be known. Trained by expensive tutors, many of these women had real talent, and some truly excellent work resulted from this welter of creativity. One collection, now housed in the British Museum, is the work of Mary Delaney (1700–1788), whose charm as a friend and hostess endeared her to such folk as Jonathan Swift, and ultimately the British royal family. Mrs Delaney was well versed in all the fashionable crazes of her day, but being less rich than her aristocratic friends, she delved deeper and more seriously into such genteel occupations as 'cut-paper work'. Her 'botanical portraits' of exotic and native flora, produced entirely from cut and tinted paper, are both wonderfully exact and meticulously executed. They also rank among the most captivating examples of botanical art extant.

Meanwhile, the craze for decoupage had also infiltrated the French court of Louis XVI. Marie Antoinette and her court ladies insouciantly snipped up the work of court painters of the calibre of Watteau, Boucher and Fragonard in their enthusiasm for decorating fans, boxes and screens. The mystery is that none of this royal decoupage seems to have survived the Revolution. Conceivably, among the offerings on a flea-market stall someone will one day discover a battered trinket box decoupaged by a royal hand.

Victorian 'scrap sheets' – mass-produced collections of colourful images – were a mid-nineteenth-century innovation that nudged decoupage into a new, wholesomely domestic phase. Making scrap screens became a popular rainy-day occupation for the nursery, allowing mamma or nanny a few hours' peace while the children snipped and pasted, messily content. Scrap work varies in artistry and execution, as one would expect. Some examples are boldly conceived and handsome, but many are a jolly jumble: animals, flowers and sentimental scenes, all mingled higgledy-piggledy with no apparent motive other than to cover every available inch.

After its Victorian heyday, decoupage experienced a decline in popularity. A few devotees, most notably Hiram Manning in the USA, made valiant attempts to revive the craft before and after the Second World War. But it took the technical innovations of the late twentieth century, such as fast-drying varnishes and the photocopying machine, to make decoupage more popular than ever.

The current practice of decoupage divides roughly into two schools of thought. Some prefer to start with black-and-white printed motifs, colouring these according to taste. Others prefer to use ready-coloured materials, ransacking wallpaper designs, wrapping papers and magazines for coloured motifs to cut out. The first approach is close in spirit and effect to the Venetian *arte povera*, and those seeking motifs to colour themselves should turn to our earlier work – *The Decoupage Sourcebook*. The second approach resembles the Victorian 'scrap' technique, and the superbly coloured pages of motifs that form the main body of this book are reproduced in this spirit, ready for use. What we have tried to do in this book is to provide the *aficionado* with enough colour-printed material of quality and variety to work endless transformations, plus sufficient practical advice to make it user friendly, and get you going with the scissors or the scalpel!

TOOLS & MATERIALS

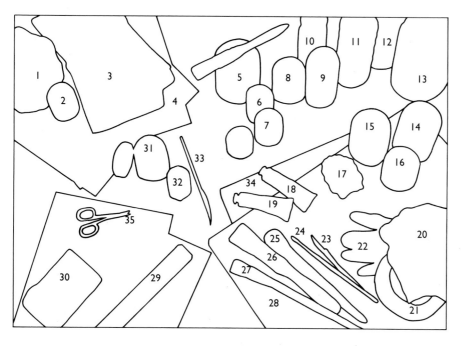

1 Wire wool 2 Gold size (water-based) 3 Dutch metal transfer leaf
4 Sandpaper and wet-and-dry paper 5 Wallpaper paste and 2.5cm (1in) brush
6 & 7 Florentine and Venetian antiquing wax 8 Button Polish (orange shellac)
9 Mulberry acrylic base paint 10 White Polish (bleached shellac) 11 Methylated spirits
12 White spirit 13 Maize acrylic base paint 14 & 15 Two-part craquelure varnish 16 PVA
17 Artist's natural sponge 18 Raw umber oil paint 19 Dark green oil paint 20 Soft rag
21 Masking tape 22 Rubber gloves 23 Scalpel 24 Fine paintbrush 25 Gilder's mop
26 2.5cm (1in) decorator's brush 27 2.5cm (1in) synthetic brush 28 Cutting mat
29 Ruler 30 Low-tack adhesive putty 31 Polyurethane varnish 32 Gold water-based
stencil paint 33 Lining brush 34 Brown paper 35 Curved manicure scissors

One of the factors that makes decoupage so accessible, to beginners especially, is that no special tools or equipment are required to carry out projects. You'll probably find that you already own several, if not all, of the items listed in this section. The most pivotal decoupage tool – a pair of scissors – is common to most households (with the bathroom cabinet usually containing a pair of fine manicure scissors for detailed work), and varnishes, sandpaper and paintbrushes often lurk in cupboards under the stairs or in makeshift tool-kits. All the items listed here can be picked up at DIY, hardware or artists' supply stores (see Suppliers, page 32) and none is costly.

The right tool can make a job easier, but there is no reason to buy everything in our picture at one go. The essentials needed for all the decoupage projects in this book are listed under Basic Equipment (see page 12). Any additional equipment required is listed on a project-by-project basis.

Source Material

The source section (see pages 33–95) includes ready-to-use colour motifs. Some are one-off images, some are duplicated for repeat designs, and others are large-scale images that would be suitable for framing. Cut out your favourites, or else you could photocopy them if you want to preserve the originals. Sourcebooks take the hard work out of decoupage, but if you enjoy hunting around for unusual or contemporary motifs, almost any type of printed material can be raided for suitable images.

Cutting Tools

The most important piece of decoupage equipment is your cutting tool, or tools. A large pair of scissors is handy for rough – and speedy – cutting out. For finer work, some people swear by good quality curved mani-cure scissors, finely pointed to let you puncture the paper on an 'inside' cut without tearing. Others are more comfortable with a scalpel and a box of refill blades. Cutting paper blunts a sharp edge quickly, so replacement blades are essential. You will also need a pair of pliers to extract used blades, and possibly a cutting mat to work on. Consider the safety aspect too – handle scalpels with care, and keep out of the reach of children.

Preparing Surfaces

To look professional, motifs should be applied to a well-prepared surface. Bare wood, papier mâché, metal and MDF (medium-density fibreboard) may only need rubbing down with abrasive paper, to smooth off roughness, followed by the appropriate primer and base paint. But a junk buy covered in old paint or varnish is best stripped down to the wood. Do this with the appropriate stripper, wearing gloves and working outdoors if possible. Brush stripper on as directed and leave paint or varnish to soften. Then, working in the direction of the wood grain, use a scraper to strip off the layers, followed by pads of medium-to-coarse wire wool to clean back to bare wood. Finish by sanding thoroughly. Cracks, knot holes and unsightly blemishes should be filled with wood filler. Fill proud, allow to dry, then sand flat.

Priming is important if your finished piece is to look really sleek. Use acrylic gesso or acrylic primer on bare wood. Both dry fast, and build up a flawless surface if you apply several coats and sand smooth in between. On metal, a metal primer will encourage paint to bond well, and will discourage rust. MDF should be sealed first with Button Polish (orange shellac) before being primed with gesso, because it is important to stop moisture entering the end grain (cut sides).

Supply yourself with several grades of abrasive papers, from coarse to fine, for rubbing back wood, and polishing primer to porcelain smoothness. Always rub back in the direction of the wood grain, never against it. Wet-and-dry paper, used with care, is nifty for smoothing paint and varnishes. Dipping the paper in water, then lightly smearing it with soap, lubricates the cutting action and helps prevent you removing too much paint or varnish at a time. Soft- and medium-grade wire wool is also good for smoothing, but dust very carefully afterwards to clear off tiny filaments.

Print Sealers and Adhesives

PVA glue, diluted with water (one part PVA to two parts water), is invaluable for 'sealing' decoupage motifs prior to cutting out. It will prevent paper from stretching, and ink from smudging. Swab on lightly with a soft brush. When the paper has dried out it may look a little wrinkled, but don't worry – once the motifs are pasted down they will appear perfectly flat. PVA can also be used for pasting down motifs. Alternatively, use ordinary wallpaper paste, which dries slowly enough to let you slide motifs around experimentally, and leaves no trace of stickiness or discoloration. A small soft sponge, squeezed out in water till moist, is useful for wiping up any PVA or paste that has leaked onto the base paint.

Varnishes

The projects described in this book make use of an unusually wide range of varnishes, which readers may find confusing if they are new to decorative painting or decoupage. It seemed helpful to categorize the different products used, and to explain why they were chosen.

It was not so long ago that varnish usually meant clear polyurethane – a tough, water-resistant, oil-based varnish sold in large quantities for general domestic use. The problem with polyurethane varnish is its propensity to darken and yellow over time, due to its linseed oil content. Professionals often prefer a more refined oil-based varnish because it yellows far less (due to the use of different oils) and because the range includes a water-clear version that dries to a completely matt – and therefore highly professional – surface, while giving useful protection.

However, whilst water-based acrylic formulations increasingly supplant the slower-drying oil-based media, a new breed of acrylic varnishes has entered the field – non-yellowing and extra-fast drying. They are undoubtedly useful, speeding up a lengthy 'finishing' process enormously (recoatable in an hour or two rather than having to be left overnight). However, these do not lend themselves to 'rubbing back' in the final stages, to achieve the super-smooth finish professional work requires, because the protective film splits and cracks off. For best results, an oil-based varnish should be used for the final one or two coats, because these are flexible enough to be smoothed with abrasive paper and wire wool to a perfectly silky finish that is tough, stain resistant and nice to handle.

If you plan to chop and change between the various varnish options (based on oil, water and spirit), it is sensible to allow different, clearly marked brushes for each, because the varnish types require completely different brush-cleaning solvents. Oil-based varnish (polyurethane) brushes must be cleaned in white spirit, water-based (acrylic) in water, and spirit-based (shellac) in methylated spirits. Getting this wrong can wreck your brush. On the whole, flat, soft-bristled brushes of the 'fitch' or 'glider' type are the best for all varnishing tasks, because they are designed to apply a fine, even coat rapidly. By contrast, standard housepainting brushes deposit too thick a coat, and tend to leave noticeable brushmarks. Colour coding, of a simple sort, is a help: dip brush handles in a paint colour, then brush the same colour on to the relevant solvent jar, for speedy reference.

Polyurethane Varnishes

These are available in matt, eggshell and gloss, and have a drying time of eight hours or overnight. They are flexible enough to rub back nicely, and resist staining by water, alcohol and coffee, so making them ideal for trays, tables, etc. They darken and yellow over time. First coats should be thinned with 5 per cent white spirit.

Refined Oil-based Varnishes

These have a similar drying time to polyurethane, but are not quite so tough. They are exceptionally easy to work with, giving smooth, level coats with noticeably fewer brushmarks, and are designed to yellow less, but they are more expensive than polyurethane. There are gloss and eggshell finishes, plus a water-clear version that is the professionals' choice for 'invisible' protection over delicate work like *trompe l'oeil*. The water-clear, dead flat, variety contains a 'flatting' agent (which provides the matt surface) and should be stirred thoroughly to distribute the agent evenly. Thin first coats with 5 per cent white spirit.

Acrylic Varnishes

These now come in many grades, from heavy duty (for floors) to moderately tough (for furniture) and light (and brittle) for small decorative items. Extra-fast drying times allow recoating on the same day. They are non-yellowing and stain resistant, and come in gloss, eggshell and matt versions. Brushmarks can be a problem, so extra-fine synthetic brushes are recommended. They are useful to build up a smooth decoupage finish fast, but should be given a final protective polyurethane coat or two, because this can be sanded back, where acrylic varnishes would split and crack off. The brushes are cleaned in water, which makes this varnish a convenient choice.

Shellac

A traditional spirit-based varnish made from a natural resin, this is still the professionals' choice for building up a deeply glossy surface, and also for isolating coats, as when a painted, absorbent finish is to be lined or otherwise treated to further decoration. A coat of shellac (one to two hours' drying time) allows mistakes to be wiped clean, without staining the base. Shellac is available as Button Polish (orange-brown), which is handy for sealing MDF prior to priming, or as White Polish (bleached shellac), which is more expensive but adds no colour to the work. Shellac should be applied with a fine brush, each coat at right angles to the previous one. It can be rubbed back successfully, but this should be done with a light hand using fine wire wool, or fine-grade wet-and-dry paper (passed first over a cake of soap), because the layers of shellac are fine and a heavy hand risks cutting back to the paint. Shellac is an excellent, traditional choice for finishing decoupage, but for protection against staining (water, alcohol), finish with one or two coats of polyurethane.

PVA

Not strictly speaking a varnish, this water-based adhesive-cum-sealant is useful for rapidly brushing over surfaces such as photocopying paper, which might react badly to standard varnishes. It goes on milky but dries clear and glossy. It should not be thought of as a 'finish', and should be given several coats of varnish. PVA is cheap, water soluble, and commonly available from DIY stores.

Waxes

These are not varnishes in the accepted sense of a permanent, protective, hard-drying film, but they are increasingly important for decorative work using state-of-the-art water-based emulsion or acrylic paints. These dry matt, and chalky looking, and professional painters (particularly of furniture) like to varnish first for protection, then wax over with clear or tinted beeswax to bring up a soft but flattering sheen. Natural beeswax barely affects the base colour, whereas tinted antiquing wax mellows and deepens it appreciably. Test first. Apply several thin coats, leave to harden, then buff with soft, clean rags.

Odds and Ends

Thin surgical gloves are handy for messy jobs like stripping paint, or sanding. Rags, preferably soft cotton, are always useful, as are clean jars with lids, sheets of old newspaper and palettes for mixing paints. A small bowl of water will keep sponges moist and fingers clean.

BASIC EQUIPMENT

The following is a list of equipment common to all the projects in this book. Start by assembling this small kit, then build up your collection of paints and varnishes as you progress.

Small curved manicure scissors or scalpel
for fine cutting
Larger scissors for rough cutting
Brushes for sealing, painting, gluing and varnishing
Wallpaper paste
PVA glue
Natural sponge
Finger bowl and water
Soft rags
Cutting mat (optional but useful)

PHOTOCOPYING

Using Photocopiers

Once you have exhausted the supply of motifs provided here, you may want to look further afield to other printed sources for more inspiration. The availability of colour photocopying means that, rather than cutting up source-books for the image that takes your fancy, you can get the page – or even just the image – reproduced in seconds, and with reasonable accuracy. Colour copying is also effective for transforming black-and-white images: at the touch of a button, they can be reproduced in the colour of your choice, or even several different colours per sheet.

Colour copying can be expensive, though, so plan to get the maximum number of images out of each sheet. Not all photocopying outlets have colour laser copiers, so check first to find out what options are available. Few individuals will have their own photocopying equipment, though anyone thinking of decoupage as a paying sideline would be well advised to investigate costs. For the occasional project, having images photocopied works out very reasonably; the days of hunting for antique prints and cutting them up guiltily are long gone.

Enlarging and Reducing Images

Whether using our motifs, or ones you have found yourself, you may want to alter the size of your motif to fit a particular item. Most small towns now have at least one studio or shop where you can have work copied to your specifications. Large images can be reduced by 50 per cent, and small images magnified by anything up to 400 per cent. Modern colour copiers offer many more sophisticated options, such as creating 'negative', white-on-black images, or making double-sided colour copies, though for the majority of decoupage projects, you will probably find that resizing is the facility you want to use most often.

Enlarging and reducing images by trial and error, until you arrive at the perfect fit for your box, vase or piece of furniture, can be costly. If you can, work out the exact magnification required before you have your motifs copied, by applying the following formula:

$$\frac{\text{The size you would like the image to be}}{\text{The size of the original}} \times 100$$

For example, to enlarge a motif that measures 7cm (3in) in length to fit a box just over 20cm (8in) long, you would need a magnification of 286% (20 ÷ 7 x 100 = 286).

Tips and Ideas

Modern photocopiers can enlarge without distortion or loss of detail. You may notice, however, if you have a great deal of photocopying done, that the ink intensity can vary quite considerably. This usually occurs when the machine ink is running out over a day's use, so try to get all your copying done in one batch.

For those on a tight budget, there are ways to cut photocopying costs. If a particular assemblage of designs is one you feel you want to repeat often, you can cut and paste down the photocopied images onto a standard A3 sheet and have it copied as many times as you need.

DAMASK ROSE
WRITING DESK

This delightful, portable writing desk harks back to the early days of decoupage, when decorated pieces would be 'japanned' with countless coats of varnish. Here the delicately coloured damask roses are set against a black background – enlivened by some discreet gilt lining – and protected by up to twenty coats of White Polish. Under the lid lies a spacious compartment for stationery.

YOU WILL NEED

Basic equipment (see page 12)
Desk in MDF or softwood
Black acrylic, fast-drying water-based paint
Damask rose motif (see page 71)
Low-tack adhesive putty
White Polish (bleached shellac)
Button Polish (orange shellac)
Gold water-based stencil paint
Flow enhancer
Fine sable lining brush
Steel straight edge
Wet-and-dry paper, fine grade
Clear, semi-sheen polyurethane varnish

1

1 Seal the desk with diluted PVA, then base paint it black, with two or three coats for good coverage. Brush each coat across the previous one, and rub back gently to smooth the surface in between coats and to help the next coat adhere.

Choose your motifs and cut them out with a scalpel (or, if you prefer, first roughly with a pair of scissors, then more carefully using sharp manicure scissors). Scalpels must be used with care, and it is best to rest your work on a self-healing cutting mat to protect your work surface.

2 Work out the best arrangement of decoupage motifs to fill the space gracefully. Use low-tack adhesive putty to hold the motifs steady while you experiment; but be careful when repositioning, because cut-outs are fragile and mending tears is a nuisance, though quite possible. Mark the motifs' final positions with pencil. Don't rush this part; take your time and experiment with lots of alternatives before making your decision.

3 Brush wallpaper paste over the back of the motifs, working carefully to avoid tearing the vulnerable

rose stalks. Also coat the part of the desk that is to be decoupaged; this will improve the bond and make for more permanent adhesion.

4 Apply the cut-outs to the surface while the paste is still damp, using the brush to smooth and press from the centre outwards to eliminate any air pockets. A soft rag can also be pressed on top to flatten out the decoupage perfectly. A scalpel can be useful for adjusting or repositioning motifs, which are fragile at this stage. Be careful only to use the flat of the blade to lift the motifs in order to avoid scratching the base coat.

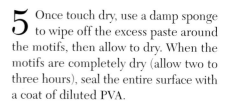

5 Once touch dry, use a damp sponge to wipe off the excess paste around the motifs, then allow to dry. When the motifs are completely dry (allow two to three hours), seal the entire surface with a coat of diluted PVA.

6 Seal the entire surface with White Polish. (We added a little Button Polish to this to give a warmer antique tone, but this is a matter of choice.) When dry, this protects the motifs and also gives a usefully smooth surface to allow the gold lining in the next stage to flow easily.

7 Use a fine, soft sable watercolour brush for the gilt lining, and a raised steel straight edge for confident brushstrokes. The paint used here is a water-based gold stencil paint, with flow enhancer added for smooth brushwork. Test the mix beforehand on a sample board (or the base of the object), to check for flow and colour density. When lining, a tip is to move your eyes a little ahead of the brush all the while. Don't worry about your ability to produce perfect lining – any wobbles can easily be wiped off with a clean, soft rag.

8 When the gilt trim is dry, seal the entire object once again with at least two coats of White Polish (or a mixture of White and Button). Four coats is better still, White Polish being so fine that with fewer coats there is a risk of 'cutting through' to the base paint and the paper motifs if you rub back too forcefully.

9 Now begin the japanner's process, smoothing and refining the sealed, decoupaged and polished surface to clear any grit or dust settling on new work, to level out brushstrokes, and to create the flawless surface of old japanning. Apply between five and twenty coats of White Polish, depending on the finish you want, and on your patience, allowing each coat to dry hard in between (two hours minimum), and smoothing each time with wet-and-dry paper. Wipe over the surface with a soft cloth before revarnishing.

For the final coats use polyurethane varnish, which will lend additional toughness, and also impermeability to the work. Keep rubbing back between coats for a flawless, satiny finish.

CABBAGE PATCH TRAY

The humble cabbage is brought centre stage on this chic breakfast tray, where a selection of curvaceous brassicas on a lime green background creates a miniature cabbage patch. The overall 'crazing' that covers the tray was achieved through the use of craquelure varnish, rubbed over with dark green oil colour. This cobweb effect helps to integrate the motifs with the base colour. Some finishing coats of tough, water-resistant varnish make this tray hard-wearing in use.

YOU WILL NEED

Basic equipment (see page 12)
Tray, approx. 45 x 35cm (18 x 14in) of wood or MDF
Button Polish (orange shellac)
Lime green emulsion paint
Cabbage motifs (see page 85)
Two-step water-based craquelure
Deep green artists' oil colour
White Polish (bleached shellac)
Clear polyurethane gloss
Wet-and-dry sandpaper, fine grade

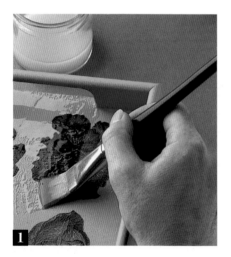

2 After one or two hours' drying time at room temperature, fine cobweb cracks will be visible when the tray is held up to the light. For rather more pronounced and dramatic results, the craquelure can be left overnight. To show up the craquelure, rub the deep green artists' oil colour in a gentle, circular action over the entire surface, using a soft rag and colour straight from the tube. The dark colour emphasizes the crackles.

1 Seal the tray with Button Polish, then paint it with two coats of lime green emulsion. Cut out the cabbage motifs, and apply them with diluted PVA (see pages 15–16). Brush the first coat of craquelure evenly over the surface of the tray, using a smaller brush to carefully get into the corners and round the handles, etc. Leave to dry naturally (about two hours) then apply the second stage of the varnish. This second coat needs to be applied very carefully, because any gaps in it will lead to unsightly streaks when the oil colour is rubbed in later.

3 Leave the oil colour to harden for an hour or two. Then, with a clean, soft rag, gently wipe off the excess oil colour, so that it remains as a fine dark network of crackles that will give an interesting texture to the decoupaged surface. Leave overnight, then seal the oil colour with a coat of fast-drying White Polish. When it is hard (two to three hours), recoat with at least two coats of tough, water-resistant polyurethane varnish. This can be lightly rubbed back with wet-and-dry after two to three coats to give it a less shiny finish.

PAINT KETTLE

I t is hard to imagine that the glamorous *cachepot* shown here, with its tracery of autumnal leaves and fruit against a glowing gilded background, started out as a humble paint kettle. Transformations are the stuff of decoupage, but somehow it is twice as exciting to make something really special from something so ordinary. Paint kettles are very cheap, sturdy, the right size to take a pot plant, and they never leak onto your best furniture.

1 Prime the paint kettle with a coat of red oxide primer followed by a coat of gold size. Thirty minutes later, gilding can begin. Press the metal leaf, still attached to its paper backing, onto the size surface, and rub firmly on the paper backing with your fingertips or with a soft, dry brush until the leaf adheres evenly to the size. Remove the backing paper. Any gaps can be patched straight away with remaining scraps of leaf. (If this fails, apply more size, wait 30 minutes, then try again.) Overlap the next metal leaf square slightly, and repeat.

Do not attempt to smooth or tidy the surface until the work is completed and has been left overnight, because at this stage the metal leaf is still fairly fragile and could easily be torn or damaged. Once it is thoroughly dry, you will then be able to perfect the finish.

2 Use a soft brush or clean rag to smooth over the gilding, detaching loose scraps and pressing the metal leaf more tightly to the base. The difference is visible, creating a smooth finish.

To 'distress' the leaf, rub gently with fine wire wool until the red oxide primer shows through here and there. Be careful not to rub so hard that you go right through the gilding to the metal. You are aiming for a gentle effect.

YOU WILL NEED

Basic equipment (see page 12)
Paint kettle
Red oxide metal primer
Gold size
6-8 sheets of Dutch metal transfer leaf
Fine wire wool
Button Polish (orange shellac)
Leaf and pear motifs (pages 83 and 87)
Two-step water-based craquelure
Raw umber artists' oil paint
White Polish (bleached shellac)

3 Cover the gold leaf with a coat of Button Polish to seal the leaf, then paste down your chosen motifs using PVA, as described on pages 15–16. Leave to dry for an hour or two. Apply two coats of craquelure varnish (see page 18) and leave to dry naturally (no hurrying with a hairdryer), followed by raw umber oil paint to reveal the cracks. Rub off the excess paint so that the colour remains only in the crackle. Leave overnight, then seal with one or two coats of White Polish. This dries shiny, but may be dulled by a gentle rubbing with wire wool after two or three coats.

PRINT
CUPBOARD

Aroom in the house of the eighteenth-century Swedish botanist Linnaeus was the inspiration for this simple but appealing decoupage project, which uses a series of botanical prints reproduced for this book. Linnaeus' room has panelled walls, and the mouldings have been used to frame a collection of contemporary botanical prints, creating a charming variant on the print room theme. Because the prints are so complete in themselves, with their coloured line borders, and rooted appearance, it seemed a pity to cut them up, especially as they fitted our cupboard panels so neatly.

YOU WILL NEED

Basic equipment (see page 12)
Panelled doors and/or wooden picture frames
Grey-green acrylic base paint
Wire wool
Print motifs (see pages 37, 41, 43 and 47)
Water-clear varnish (see page 11)
Plain and tinted beeswax

an easy and effective way of livening up the matt, rather chalky appearance of water-based emulsion-type paints.

2 Use another soft clean rag to wipe off excess wax so that only a veil of antiquing colour remains, especially over the prints themselves. The previous PVA seal and varnish enable this to be done without detriment to the paper cut-outs. A further application of wax on the painted surfaces allows these to be polished up by gentle rubbing, giving a mellow sheen that is reminiscent of eighteenth-century Scandinavian paintwork.

1 First give the cupboard two coats of base paint, then lightly rub them down with wire wool to smooth the surface. Select your prints and paste them carefully onto the panels with diluted PVA (see pages 15–16), then, when they are in position, brush more of this diluted PVA over the prints to seal them. Varnish the whole cupboard – prints included – for protection against scuffs and stains.

With a soft rag, rub a mixture of plain and tinted beeswax over the entire surface, prints included, with an extra-heavy application of tinted wax going onto the panel mouldings. Soft waxes provide

3 The framed print opposite shows how effective a single print can look, when mounted in ivory card and framed with a simple wooden frame, painted to match the cupboard. A group of such framed prints would look fresh and appealing. Quite a few framing shops now provide a DIY framing service, which greatly reduces the cost of the exercise. They cut and mitre the unfinished mouldings, and supply glass, mounting board, etc; you do the rest. A whole set of prints framed in this way can work out hardly more expensive than getting a single print framed professionally.

BLOOMING BOOKENDS

Our little clumps of hellebores are so charming, and their shape so chubbily complete, that the challenge was to find a suitable pair of objects to display them to advantage. The pair of MDF bookends we used were tailor-made for the project. MDF is ideally suited to small decorative pieces like these, as it lends itself especially well to fancy outlines and smoothly carved mouldings, needing no filling and prepping, unlike cheap softwoods. It may need a preliminary coat of Button Polish before painting begins, to seal the surface and prevent the paint soaking in. The pale blue bookends have been given a decorative dragged effect through the application of some ultramarine-tinted glaze.

Lining – that is, painting fine lines for emphasis with a lining brush – is a traditional means of setting off painted pieces. In the old days, liners were a recognized group of skilled painters, able to whip off fine, almost calligraphic, freehand brushwork, straight as a die. Replete with twirly flourishes, it crisped up and emphasized anything from the bodywork of royal coaches to the edges of a papier mâché tray. Many professional painters fight shy of lining, but no one need feel nervous of attempting it on small pieces like our bookends, or even the larger writing desk (see page 14).

YOU WILL NEED

Basic equipment (see page 12)
MDF bookends
Button Polish (orange shellac)
Pale blue acrylic base paint
Hellebore motifs (see page 79)
Acrylic glaze
Ultramarine acrylic tube colour
Wet-and-dry paper
White Polish (bleached shellac)
White acrylic colour
Flow enhancer
Fine sable lining brush
Clear gloss polyurethane varnish

1 Seal the MDF with Button Polish, and leave to dry, then paint the bookends with pale blue acrylic base paint. Cut out the hellebore motifs, and paste in place with diluted PVA (see pages 15 –16). When dry, clean off excess PVA and seal with more PVA or White Polish.

To give the pieces a quick, easy version of the traditional decorative dragged effect, use an acrylic glaze, tinted a few shades darker than the base paint with the ultramarine tube colour, and brush it over the whole surface, following an imagined grain direction. Once it has set for ten minutes or so, distress it by rubbing back the glaze

over the decoupage motifs with wet-and-dry to leave just a trace of colour. Apply a second, darker, coat of glaze over the mouldings to give them prominence.

2 Coat the bookends with another coat of fast-drying White Polish. For the lining, use a fine sable brush, and mix flow enhancer into the white acrylic to enable the brushstroke to cover the distance in one. Stopping and starting is what makes lining look clumsy. When the lines are finished, and the corners neatly defined, give the bookends two coats of clear gloss polyurethane varnish for protection.

STRIPY TULIP WASTEBIN

1 Mask off the metal bin for a striped finish, using strips of masking tape stuck down at regular intervals round the bin, and stretched taut from top to bottom. (Perfectionists with a mathematical bent may wish to measure the bin's circumference to determine the precise spacing of the stripes; lazies will do this by eye, placing tapes a touch closer or further apart on the home lap, knowing that fractional differences will be lost in the end result.) Spray the bin all over with short bursts of spray paint. Unless your room is well-ventilated, do this spraying outside to avoid a build-up of fumes.

A perfectly plain metal wastebin, like an overgrown tin can, gets a dazzling stripy background to floral decoupage, using thin masking tape and spray paint. Although it is a bit fiddly, this striping technique is easy to do and gives highly professional results. The trick is to run a thumbnail down both sides of the tape to ensure that spray colour does not creep under the tape to give a fuzzy outline. The visual interest here lies in the contrast between the shiny metal and the matt black stripes, against which the gorgeous tulips form a bright splash of colour.

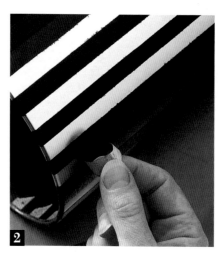

YOU WILL NEED

Basic equipment (see page 12)
Metal wastebin
1cm (½in) masking tape
Spray paint
Tulip motifs (see page 35)
Sheet of blotting paper
Clear matt or eggshell
polyurethane varnish

2 Leave the spray paint to harden for a while before peeling off the masking tape strips. This is always an exciting moment, when the 'negative' design becomes 'positive'. Don't worry about any slight imperfections or wobbles as they can easily be removed. On a smooth metal ground, as here, smudged edges are quite easily tidied by being scraped off with a sharp scalpel blade. On a painted surface, a fuzzy outline is best tidied with a fine brush dipped in the base paint. Finicky though this may seem, it is worth the effort, as the gain in slickness is visible.

3 Arrange your decoupage motifs so that you are happy with the effect, then stick them in place with diluted PVA (see pages 15–16). Use a sheet of blotting paper to blot up any surplus moisture and leaking PVA around the motifs. This is optional, but saves time on cleaning up operations before the final protective varnishing. (Although PVA dries to a transparent finish, it can show through as a faintly altered texture in the end result.)

Coat the bin inside and out with a tough polyurethane varnish for protection, choosing matt or eggshell, depending on your preference.

POPPY LAMP BASE

The Victorians used to paste pretty coloured scraps inside little glass bottles before filling them with sand, or salt, to make attractive keepsakes. We adapted this ruse on a much larger scale for a sturdy glass storage jar, and substituted spray paint for sand, to make a colourful lamp base with a 1960s air. Handsome old sweet jars, minus their lids, often turn up at boot sales, and this simple technique could give them a new lease of life. Make sure that your jar's neck is wide enough to get your hand in and out.

YOU WILL NEED

Basic equipment (see page 12)
Scouring pad
Large glass storage jar, as wide-necked and heavy as possible
Poppy motifs (see pages 75 and 77)
Thick paper
Masking tape
Spray paint
Electric lamp fitting

1 Make sure your jar is perfectly clean, using a scouring pad if necessary to remove old grime. Dry thoroughly. Try the effect of different motif shapes, colour combinations, arrangements, etc., by sliding them in and holding in place. You might prefer a ring of tall-stemmed flowers, or a scatter of small motifs. There is a vast selection of motifs provided at the end of the book from which to choose. Paint the inside of the jar where the motifs will be placed, and also the fronts of the motifs, with diluted PVA. Slide each motif in carefully (they are fragile when wet) and press firmly, right side out, onto the glass. Use your fingertips or a clean rag to remove any air bubbles. Be very gentle, so that there is no danger of tearing the flowers as you smooth them.

2 Leave the gummed motifs for an hour or so to dry securely, then, with a damp rag or sponge, work round them to remove as much as possible of the PVA, being careful not to rub so hard that you lift the pasted motifs. If this happens, use a fine brush to slip a touch more PVA into the lifted area, press down and leave to dry, then continue.

3 Now you are ready to spray paint your jar. Tape a protective collar of thick paper round the neck of the jar and down its 'shoulders' outside, to save cleaning later, and do your spraying out of doors to avoid any build up of toxic fumes. Spray a few short bursts, leave to settle, check for coverage and repeat as necessary. Leave to dry overnight then remove the protective collar. Sandwiched between glass and paint, your decoupage will look stunning and professional.

To turn your decorated jar into a lampbase, ask an electrician or lighting expert to wire it up for you.

SUNFLOWER BOX FILE

YOU WILL NEED

Basic equipment (see page 12)
Papered box file
Flower motifs (see pages 49 and 53)
Steel straight edge
Matt acrylic varnish

Here we show how to transform a box file from the drably functional to something so individual and colourful that the chore of filing those endless documents loses some of its sting. Decoupaged stationery also makes cheap and cheerful presents. A keen gardener would enjoy keeping garden notes or catalogues in a pretty box file like the one shown here.

Colour provided a theme for the motifs we chose, from the warm orange and terracotta of the polyanthus and sunflower to the dark crimson of the berries.

2 Stick the main body of the sunflower to the lid of the file with diluted PVA, and wrap it over the edge so that the motif carries on visually. Slice off along the lower edge of the lid. Offer up the other half of the motif to the side of the box to determine just where it should be stuck in order to continue the image unbroken. Pencil marks help with accurate positioning. Stick the stalk and leaves in their place, and fine-tune their positions. (PVA allows a little play before the adhesive grips, which is why it is such a good choice for decoupage.) Precise lining up of bisected motifs like this may

1 Covering lidded items invariably means that some motifs will spill over from the tops to the sides. When this happens, you need to cut the motifs in question and join them invisibly where the lid meets the side. Done carefully, this can be almost seamless, and looks very sleek and professional.

Arrange your flower motifs until you are happy with them, then take any flower that flows from the top down to the side (in this case the sunflower) and assess where the critical cut will be. Use a scalpel and a straight edge to make the cut, resting on a cutting mat for safety.

seem a small detail, but you will find that taking the time and effort to get it right adds considerably to the final effect.

Seal the box file thoroughly with PVA, followed by a coat or two of matt varnish for protection.

It is easy to make more of an idea like this, decoupaging a range of additional desk paraphernalia to match. Another possibility might be to concentrate on the backs of a whole set of box files, using tall-stemmed floral motifs, so that when lined up on a shelf or window sill they look like a herbaceous border. Never again will filing seem tedious.

SUPPLIERS

UNITED KINGDOM

J W Bollom
121 South Liberty Lane, Ashton Vale, Bristol
Tel: 0117 966 5151
Varnishes, craquelure, gilding materials, glues, shellac, gesso, artists' oil paints, brushes. Delivery service from eight nationwide brances.

Cornelisson and Son
105 Great Russell Street, London WC1B 3LX
Tel: 0171 636 1045
Fax: 0171 636 3655
A full range of decoupage tools and materials. Mail order.

The Dover Bookshop
18 Earlham Street, London
Tel: 0171 836 2111
Fax: 0171 836 1603
Decoupage sourcebooks. Catalogue available. Mail order.

Fiddes and Sons
Florence Works, Bridley Road, Cardiff
Tel: 0122 234 0323
Varnishes, craquelure, glues, shellac, emulsion paints, brushes, metal primer. Mail order.

W Habberley Meadows
5 Saxon Way, Chelmsley Wood, Birmingham B37 5AY
Tel: 0121 770 2905

A full range of tools and materials.

A S Handover
Angel Yard, Highgate, High Street, London N6 5JU
Tel: 0181 340 0665
Cutting tools, varnishes, craquelure, gilding materials, glues, gesso, shellac, artists' paints, watercolours. Mail order.

John T Keep and Sons
15 Theobalds Road, London WC1X 8SL
Tel: 0171 242 7578
Cutting tools, varnishes, gilt cream, glues, shellac, emulsion paints, artists' oil paints, brushes, metal primer.

London Graphic Centre
107-115 Long Acre, London WC2E 9NT
Tel: 0171 240 0095
A large range of artists' materials, including acrylic and oil paints, paintbrushes and gilding materials.

E Milner
Glanville Road, Cowley, Oxford OX4 2DB
Tel: 0186 571 8171
Cutting tools, varnishes, craquelure, gilding materials, glues, shellac, gesso, emulsions, brushes. Mail order.

John Myland Ltd
80 Norwood High Street, London SE27 9NW
Tel: 0181 670 9161
Varnishes, craquelure, glues, gilt cream, shellac, gesso, emulsion paints, brushes. Mail order.

John Oliver Paints & Wallpapers
33 Pembridge Road, London W11 3HG
Tel: 0171 221 6466
Emulsion paints. Mail order.

Paint Magic
116 Sheen Road, Richmond, Surrey TW9 1UR
Tel: 0181 940 5503
Tools, books, motifs, materials. Paint Magic paints.

E Ploton Ltd
273 Archway Road, London N6 5AA
Tel: 0181 348 0315
Cutting tools, varnishes, craquelure, gilding materials, shellac, gesso, artists' paints, watercolours, brushes. Mail order, except for inflammable or toxic items.

Stuart Stevenson
68 Clerkenwell Road, London EC1
Tel: 0171 253 1693
Cutting tools, varnishes, craquelure, gilding materials, glues, shellac, gesso, artists' paints, watercolours, brushes, metal primer. Mail order.

AUSTRALIA

The Folk Art Studio,
200 Pittwater Road, Manly, NSW 2095
Tel: 02 9977 7091
A full range of decoupage tools and materials

Handworks Supplies
121 Commercial Road, South Yarra, Victoria 3181
Tel: 03 9820 8399
Stockists of general art and craft supplies.

Janet's Art Supplies and Art Books
145 Victoria Avenue, Chatswood 2067, Sydney
Tel: 02 417 8572
Decoupage kits and 'scraps'.

Paper 'N' Things
88 Union Street, Armadale, Victoria 3143
Tel: 03 9576 0223
A full range of decoupage materials.

CANADA

Coast Decorating Centre
4464 Main Street, Vancouver, BC, VSV 3R3
Tel: 604 872 5275
Brushes and decorating tools, natural sponges, glazes, paints.

Day's Painting Supplies
10733 104 Avenue, Edmonton, AB, T5J 3K1

Tel: 403 426 4848
Natural sponges, glazes and special paints.

Maiwa Supplies
6-1666 Johnston Street, Vancouver, BC V6H 3S2
Tel: 604 669 3939
Decoupage materials.

Mona Lisa Artists' Materials
1518 7th Street, SW, Calgary, AB, T2R 1A7
Tel: 403 228 3618
A wide range of decoupage and artists' materials.

Nautilus Arts & Crafts Inc.
6057 Kingston Road, Westhill, ON, M1C 1K5
Tel: 416 284 1171
Prints and decoupage materials.

New York Paint & Wallpaper
1704 Clair Avenue, West Toronto, ON, M6N 1J1
Tel: 416 656 2223
A full range of decorating supplies, including sea sponges and glazes.

Paint Magic
101, 1019 17th Avenue, SW, Calgary, AB, T2T 0A7
Tel: 403 245 6866
Stockists of a full range of Paint Magic paints, plus decoupage prints, books, tools and materials.

Western Paint and Wallcovering Co. Ltd
521 Hargrave Street, Winnipeg, MB, R3A 0Y1
Tel: 204 942 7271
Paints and glazes.

White Rose
4400 Dufferin Street, North York, ON, M3H 5R9
Tel: 416 663 4172
Decoupage tools and materials.

SOUTH AFRICA

The following outlets supply a wide range of decoupage and artists' tools and materials.

Art Book Centre
Sandton Place, Corner of Elizabeth & 10th Street, Parkmore, Johannesburg
Tel: 011 883 5304

Barney's Paint Centre
Fourways Shopping Centre, Sandton, Shop 3, Entrance 5, Johannesburg
Tel: 011 465 6490

Crafty Supplies
32 Main Road, Claremont Cape
Tel: 021 610 286

P W Story (Pty) Ltd
18 Foundry Lane, Durban
Tel: 031 306 1224

Wardkiss Homecare DIY Superstores
Blue Route Shopping Centre, PO Box 30094, Tokai Cape
Tel: 021 725 000

PLUMERIA, flore rosea odoratissime. Inst. R.H. app. 659.

41

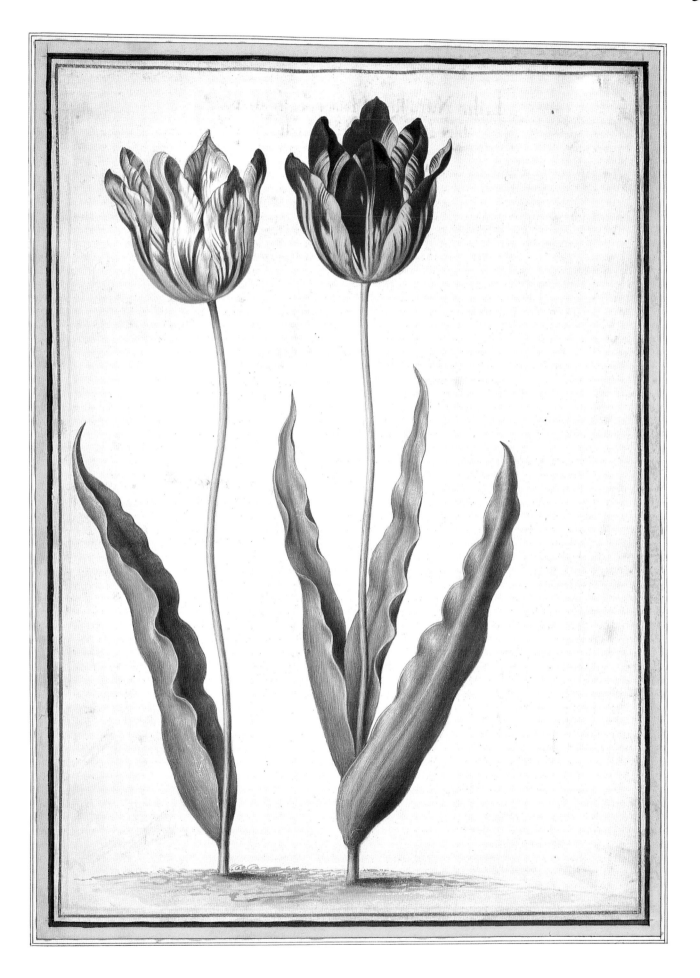

N. 371.

Chrysanthemum Indicum flore et semine maximum,
Sonnen-blum.

H.

Helleborus niger,
Orientalis, amplissimo
folio, caule praealto,
flore viridi, Itineris
Tournefort.

MAGNOLIA altissima Lauro Cerasi folio flore ingenti candide
The Laurel leav'd Tulip tree.

59